FOR YOUTH MINISTRY

Sunday School CPR

How to Breathe New Life Into Sunday Morning

by Fred Edie

ABINGDON PRESS

Nashville, Tennessee

About the Writer

Fred Edie has worked in youth ministry for the past eighteen years. He is at work on a Ph.D. in Religious Education at Emory University. He teaches a senior high Sunday school class that he says students would say is "almost tolerable." Fred is married to Alison Hester Edie (who also finds him almost tolerable), and has two young children

Acknowledgments

The Holy Spirit; Professor Charles Foster, Candler School of Theology, Emory University, whose character as a teacher has helped to shape my own life; John Gooch, pastor, writer, editor, and long-time teacher of youth; Flo Sapp Martin, curriculum consultant, Sunday school teacher, parent of a teenager; Meg Procopio, who is proving her leadership with an effective Christian education program; Crys Zinkiewicz, editor extraordinaire, Sunday school teacher, lover of youth.

SKILLABILITIES FOR YOUTH WORKERS
Sunday School CPR
How to Breathe New Life Into Sunday Morning
Volume 9

ISBN 0-687-08690-6

98 99 00 01 02 03 04 05 06—10 9 8 7 6 5 4 3 2 1

EDITORIAL AND DESIGN TEAM
Editor: Crystal A. Zinkiewicz
Production Editor: Sheila K. Hewitt
Design Manager: Phillip D. Francis
Designer: Sheila K. Hewitt
Cover Design: Diana Maio
& Phillip D. Francis

ADMINISTRATIVE TEAM
Publisher: Neil M. Alexander
Vice President: Harriett Jane Olson
Executive Editor, Teaching and Study Resources: Duane A. Ewers
Editor of Youth Resources: M. Steven Games

CONTENTS

A 60-Second Course in Church History

Sunday school as we know it is a relatively recent (18th and 19th centuries) innovation in the life of our 2000-year-old church. But...

the church has always been
about the business
of making disciples
of Jesus Christ.

Preparation for baptism in the early church included a three-year period of spiritual discipline and teaching. Candidates for baptism learned in detail the biblical story of salvation and discovered what allegiance to Christ and his church would mean for their lives.

In eighteenth-century England, a practical-minded Anglican priest named John Wesley organized members of his Methodist movement into small groups for mutual support in Christian living. Group members promised to use the means of grace, including regular searching of the Scriptures.

Wesley also noted that parish priests were not instructing children, so he instructed his preachers to teach the children in their charges.

Robert Raikes, a newspaper publisher, who was concerned for poor, unchurched children, established the first official Sunday school in 1780 in England. He made a virtue out of a necessity—Sunday was the only day that children were not at work in the factories!

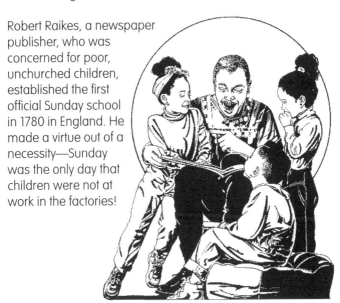

In the late 1800s, Mary McLeod (later, Bethune), who co-founded the historically African-American Bethune-Cookman College, in Florida, established Sunday school for the poorest children in Augusta, Georgia. Though some laws at that time were finally protecting children from exploitative labor practices, there was no rest for their weary parents, who were forced to work even on Sundays. The all-day Sunday school provided a safe environment for children and youth while teaching equal measures of

song and Scripture, health and hygiene, self-reliance and responsibility.

Sunday school has always been a creative, adaptive response on the part of the church to different situations that threatened the spiritual vitality of its people. Now, when some people think that Sunday school has outlived its usefulness, we need to be careful not to confuse the means with the ends.

Our goal must always be the formation of youth as faithful disciples of Jesus Christ.

Today the means to this end may include breathing new life into the Sunday school, but the means may also include practical ways to transform, and even transcend, Sunday school.

An Equally Short Course in Theology

The Church teaches
—in response to God's offer of salvation by way of baptism into the life, death, and resurrection of Jesus Christ;
    —out of gratitude for this saving gift and the desire to share it with the world;
    —because we recognize that our baptism requires of us a new way of living.

Sunday school is a forum for telling the stories of God that help us identify ourselves as people of God's baptismal covenant. These stories are

found in the Bible,
    in church tradition,
        and in the individual
memories of church members.

If you forget the stories, you'll lose your identity, you'll fall out of covenant. It's as simple as that.

Sunday school is a place where the stories of who we are as Covenant People bump up against the realities of our society and culture, our past and present.

Old stories, even the biblical ones, are just so many dusty books if they are not written into the narrative of our current lives.

In Sunday school, we can ask the "so what?" questions, the "what does this mean for us right now?" questions of our faith and tradition.

Sunday school is an important setting for learning about worship. Worship is crucial because, first and foremost, it is what Christians do. In worship, mind, body, and heart are formed into the character of a disciple of Jesus. The power of God to meet and form a people through worship depends in part on the response of the people.

Sunday school is a place to learn how to praise God rightly. Our capacity to worship may be innate, but it must also be nurtured.

Sunday school is a laboratory for Christian living. It is a place to discover that Christian faith is a community project. On the one hand, we are not alone in our search for faith; and on the other hand, we are stuck with one another. Youth especially need the fellowship, nurture, and accountability that a positive Christian peer group provides.

Sunday school is a place where teens can also to come to terms with conflict and diversity peacefully. They can learn to treat with decency and compassion persons who have not yet made their top ten list.

A Bonus Elective in Developmental Assets

Search Institute has identified **40 key assets** that contribute to the health and wholeness of young persons both now and in their futures. Sunday school can provide several of them.

OTHER ADULT RELATIONSHIPS   Asset #3
Youth require a variety of adult models and mentors to assist them on the journey to adulthood.

SAFETY   Asset #10
We're not talking just physical safety here (though we would certainly hope that church attendance is not life threatening!); we're also talking about a sanctuary for the spirit, where feelings of doubt and struggle will be treated with compassion and trust. As one teacher puts it, Sunday school is a place where you can "ask anything you want, anytime you want, and no one will ever put you down for asking something you really want to know the answer to." (John Gooch, "Making Sunday School Come Alive," *YouthNet*, Summer 1997, page 3)

INTEGRITY
Asset #28

Youth develop this virtue as faith becomes integral to their lives.

RESISTANCE SKILLS
Asset #35

An effective Sunday school class makes possible orientation to a positive peer group, which is essential for the formation of character capable of resisting the destructive, risk-taking behaviors of negative peer groups.

SENSE OF PURPOSE
Asset #39

Disciples of Jesus carry with them hope for the future and a trajectory for a life.

What Does the Bible Say?

A quick spin through a biblical concordance reveals no listings for Sunday school. So far as we know, Jesus never said, "Establish a school-like institution on what one day will become the Christian sabbath in remembrance of me."

But, even if there were no Sunday school in Bible days, there were strong connections between teaching and faithfulness.

The core of Israel's faith was what God had done through their ancestors. So **it was crucial to know the stories.**

Joshua 4 reminds us of the importance of passing on the stories to new generations.

Deuteronomy 6:4–8 says that Israel is not only to keep the Great Commandment, but to diligently teach it to the children and talk about it. There were to be constant physical reminders of God's saving activity as well.

Teaching was never for its own sake (or to score big at that evening's campfire Levitical Trivial Pursuit competition). **The purpose of teaching was to form a faithful people.**

This is why Jeremiah longed for the day when God's Law would be written upon people's hearts (**Jeremiah 31:31–34**). Knowledge was not enough; the new covenant would be based on the commitment of the whole person in gratitude and obedience to God.

Jews (males at least) studied God's Word together and in the company of master scholars. Jesus learned the Scripture and the traditions of his people in the synagogue.

After Paul preached in the synagogue at Beroea, the Beroeans examined the Scriptures every day to see if these things Paul claimed about Jesus were so (**Acts 17:11b**).

An Ethiopian eunuch (**Acts 8:26–39**), bewildered by a passage in Isaiah, asked Philip to help him understand what he was reading.

So, there are three biblical connections with the Sunday school:

1. It is important to pass on to new generations the **stories of the faith.**
2. The point of study is **right living before God.**
3. Knowledge of God is a not a solo task but **work done in community.**

SUNDAY SCHOOL CHECK-UP

When a patient seeks medical treatment, the doctor or nurse always begins by taking a medical history, assessing vital signs, and examining the patient before offering diagnosis and treatment. We need to do this with the Sunday school as well.

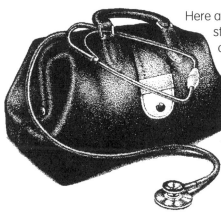

Here are some simple steps to checking out the Sunday school patient. (Note: This is checkup stuff. In the material that follows, you will find suggestions for both CPR and long-range health for your Sunday school.)

Taking the History; Checking Vital Signs

Attendance

What is the current youth enrollment and attendance in Sunday school? What are the 5- and 10-year trends in enrollment and attendance? Do these trends match the trends in public school enrollment? trends in the number of youth listed in census data?

Your church should have records of this kind. Don't settle for impressions and opinions; **get the data.**

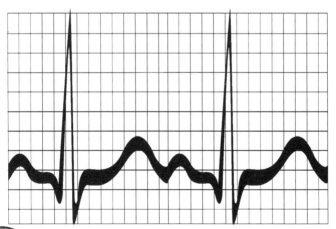

Organization

How is youth Sunday school structured? Do youth have their own classes? Are these classes divided into middle school and high school? by individual age level? Is the current class organization different from the recent past? If so, how and why?

Teachers

Who are the teachers? How are they identified and called to the task? How are they trained or supported? How long do they serve? What are their perceived strengths and weakness?

Logistics

When and where does youth Sunday school meet? What are the advantages and disadvantages of the current place and time? Are there opportunities other than on Sunday morning for Sunday school for youth who cannot attend at the traditional time?

Curriculum

Does your congregation (or denomination) have a long-range plan for helping youth learn and practice the faith? Do youth classes use published curriculum resources? Are they from denominational or independent sources? What are the perceived strengths and weaknesses of the current plan? of the resources?

Examining the Patient

Survey youth and adult leaders about Sunday school, using the questions on pages 22–23. Use this in addition to the demographic data you already have.

In addition to a survey, do personal interviews with a selection of students and teachers. Their responses can help flesh out hard data with the richness of real-life experience. Think of the interviews as a gesture of pastoral concern from the church. People appreciate being listened to.

Do you agree or disagree? Mark the following statements, using a scale of 1 to 4, with 1 representing strong agreement and 4 representing strong disagreement.

A. The purposes of youth Sunday school are

___to teach how the Bible and church tradition are important to my faith

___to discuss current issues important to me and how they relate to Christianity

___to call people into a saving relationship with Jesus Christ

___to learn about and have opportunities for worship

___to provide a safe place where I can trust others with my joys and struggles

___to be with friends

___to keep youth out of trouble

___to keep youth coming to church

B. Using the same scale as in Section A, rank how effectively your Sunday school class accomplishes the purposes that you've identified with a 1 or 2.

C. Complete the following sentences:

A subject I'd like to cover in Sunday school is

If I could choose the ideal time and place for my class to meet, it would be

What I value about Sunday school is

One way I would improve youth Sunday school is

DIAGNOSES, TREATMENTS, YOUR WELLNESS PLAN

Together, as a concerned community, review the information gathered. At first, you may have only more questions. Good! Talk about how you will find answers. Uncover assumptions. Look at perceptions from a different angle.

What trends do you see in the data? Are demographic boomlets squeezing the other age levels? Is there a need for a new class or a redistribution of educational resources, including teachers, space, and so forth?

Are teachers, curriculum, meeting time and place, perceived purposes judged to be strengths or weaknesses in youth Sunday school? Are youth facilities, for example, located in a geographical (or metaphorical) Babylon far away from the important centers of communal life? What does this facilities exile communicate to youth? (See page 45 for more on the Unspoken Curriculum.)

Do youth and adults see the purpose and effectiveness of youth Sunday school alike or differently? If they see them differently, what does this suggest as a possible next step?

Perception: The school image doesn't play well with the MTV crowd.
Another View: School is not a four-letter word. (And you can thank a teacher that you know it.)

Boomer memories of boring lectures and snoring students are not necessarily an accurate picture of today. Teaching is far more interactive, cooperative, and technology driven.

Youth grumble about school the way adults complain about their jobs. The truth is that the majority do well in school and enjoy being part of a community of creativity and learning.

 Do your teachers use learning activities?

Perception: Sunday school is way too formal and overstructured compared with fellowship groups.
Another View: Not everybody wants to be part of the Kum-Ba-Yah crowd!

Rx Youth learn in more than one way and feel comfortable in more than one setting. Does your Sunday school provide for the **various learning styles and interests** of your youth?

Perception: Kids are comatose on Sunday morning.
Another View: And they're not comatose Monday through Friday mornings?

True, youth are out late Saturday night partying or cleaning up the Burger Doodle or staying up for whatever is on after *Saturday Night Live*. And true, adolescents require more sleep than adults and generally more than they are getting. But the Sunday school is not at any greater disadvantage than the regular school in this regard.

Rx **Consider food.** Note that adult classes usually have to have their coffee!

Rx **Change the time.** The sacred has to do with transforming youth into the image of Jesus Christ, not with keeping traditional times and settings.

Perception: Kids would rather be grocery shopping with their grandmas than sit through Sunday school.
Another View: Everybody's gotta eat!

Youth Sunday school is often populated by an interesting combination of youth. Some enjoy church and are present whenever the door's open; others are there because they have to! This latter group consists of "the least, the last, and the lost" for whom Jesus came. There is no other constituency more deserving or more needful of the most compassionate ministry the church has to offer.

So why would they rather be grocery shopping? What's missing in the Sunday school? Why aren't they comfortable—or excited—about being there? Here's a radical idea: **Why not ask them?** Tell them that you're concerned and really want honest answers. (And if you re going to get defensive, have someone else do the asking!)

Rx for a Wellness Plan

Emergency rooms and CPR deal with immediate crises. True health means attention to lifestyles. (Yeah, diet, exercise, rest, all that jazz.)

The elements listed below are not quick fixes or emergency room treatment. They are about long-term care. See pages 47–61 for emergency treatment.

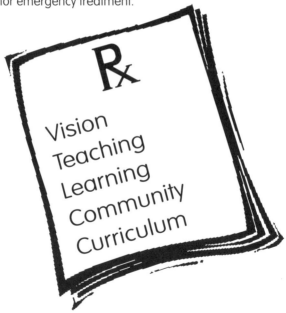

Rx

Vision
Teaching
Learning
Community
Curriculum

Vision

If you don t know where you want to go, any path will get you there.

What is the vision you hold for youth Sunday school? Go back to the list of purposes on the survey (pages 22–23). Is there a clear sense of destination? Some things are important milestones upon the path.

But where do you want to go?
Create a vision statement
together.

> My vision of what I do in youth Sunday school is help build more faithful disciples. I try to do that by teaching the faith, teaching the Bible, teaching critical thinking skills, and building community.
>
> —John Gooch

Teaching as Calling

In spite of occasional bouts of twisted-arm syndrome, most youth teachers know that they are called by God to a vital ministry of the church. Teaching is a way to express gratitude for their baptismal gift, a way to give back to God a measure of the grace they have received.

Teaching as Craft

Excellent teachers of youth bring more to the task of teaching than faithfulness to God. In fact, precisely because they are faithful, they are also motivated to acquire the tools, techniques, and skills of their craft. (In case you're wondering, there are bagsful of skills in the sections to follow.) Teachers as crafts persons are always looking for better ways to understand the faith, the youth they teach, and how to make connections between the two.

Teaching as Art

Sunday school teaching becomes art when, in the power and presence of the Spirit of God, students are moved to a fresh insight or a new perspective. They are inspired to a new vision of what is possible for their lives with God.

Teaching becomes art
when students are empowered
to sing the Christian faith
in the key of their own lives.

Teaching as Being

A culture in a hurry tends to skip the being part of teacher and gets right to the doing. But the teacher's character counts.

The number one ingredient for a successful Sunday school: A teacher who cares.

—From an informal survey of youth

Youth will forgive a host of methodological misfires if they sense the teacher to be the real deal—that is, authentically Christian. To employ the classical language, a teacher who is a Christ carrier for youth will teach through his or her life far more powerfully than any weekly lesson could.

People remember teachers not subjects.

Learning: More Than Information

Sunday school is formation because it is more than intellectual engagement with its subject matter. It seeks to form the character of individual and corporate life.

At its best, Sunday school equips students' hearts, minds, and bodies with the skills, virtues, and habits of character to live faithfully as disciples of Jesus.

As descriptively strong as formation is, it contains a blind spot—it assumes that the community doing the forming is an ideal one. Given that we're not ideal, we remember a God who is making all things new. In and through our inadequate teaching, youth gain skills, virtues, and habits of character that enable them to transform their personal and communal life ever more faithfully into the pattern of Christ.

To be "formed" into the character of Jesus so that they may then participate in God's "transformation" of their lives and the world,

youth must be nurtured in the skills for "making meaning."

As Charles Foster suggests in his book *Educating Congregations: The Future of Christian Education* (Abingdon, 1994), making meaning is more than,

"recalling" a Bible passage and "applying" it to your life.

Making meaning requires skills for critical reflection on the resources of Christian faith (Scripture, tradition, liturgy, service, and so forth) as well as on the social, cultural, and historical situation in which youth find themselves.

Youth learn to ask difficult questions of their faith tradition and current life. In the process, they come to recognize that they must also answer equally difficult questions posed by their faith tradition and current life.

What might teaching for meaning-making look like in a classroom? Take the Book of Jonah, for example. Thoughtful youth will be saying (the braver ones aloud), "Give me a break. This didn't really happen. What's going on here?"

OK, good so far. Youth are thinking abstractly and critically. So that simple (to some teachers, blasphemous) question symbolizes a whole lot of other questions:

What is the relationship between truth and fact?

Is science the only credible method for discovering truth?

Is the Bible's authority dependent on its historical verifiability?

Is the story still true if Jonah wasn't real?

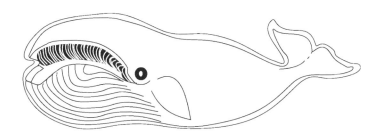

Sometimes teaching for meaning-making by raising difficult questions will require youth to unlearn old ways of knowing so that they may step into new ones.

But freed from issues of acidity and oxygen counts in fish guts, students may finally be invited into the world of text and author. Then they can begin to see Jonah as a protest against a people who thought that being chosen meant to exclude everyone else. What God was really saying was that the chosen people should include everyone else, even their enemies!

A key question always is "what did the author of the text mean by it?" **But teaching for meaning-making does not stop here.**

As the meaning of the biblical account becomes clearer, students may be invited to view their own community, church, nation, and even themselves from the perspective of the text. According to Stephen E. Fowl and L. Gregory Jones, authors of *Reading in Communion: Scripture and Ethics in Christian Life*, students learn to "be read by Scripture" as well as to read Scripture. In doing so, they learn to see themselves as others (including the Scriptures) see them. Jonah's story challenges them to look for signs of pride of place, running from responsibility, or active rebellion against God in their own communities and lives.

The point of learning
to make meaning
is not only to see clearly
but **to do something.**

Meaning-making provides a creative and faithful way of seeing the world in order to more creatively and faithfully be in the world as disciples of Jesus. Skills for making meaning form youth as better hearers and better doers of the Word.

From Class to Community

Learning is a communal project. But how do strangers become a community? The obvious answer is that creation of Christian community is a gift of the Holy Spirit. But how might we assist the Spirit in this transformation?

Teacher-Student Relationships

—Teachers can ask friendly questions: Where do you go to school? What year? Extracurricular activities? Job? Summer, Christmas plans? After school, what next?

—Birthdays, prolonged absences, public recognition for excellence by the local media, and so forth provide excuses for cards, phone calls, and other friendly contact.

—A teacher's occasional attendance at sporting events
   and arts performances or patronage of the local
   Burger Doodle employment center communicates to
   students care for the whole of their lives.

Student-Student Relationships

Students in your class don't necessarily know one another.
They may go to different schools and live in different
neighborhoods.

—Mixers, non-threatening activities that get them moving
   around and talking to one another help break the ice
   (thus, their equally clever designation as ice breakers).
   Most curriculum resources incorporate mixers. Use them;
   they are after more than fun and games.

—Teaching methods that foster student discussion,
   participation, and cooperation help students know and
   trust one another. In other words, do something other than
   lecture. A simple "nudge your neighbor and talk" or
   breaking into small groups of three or four for a brief
   response to a question energizes discussion *and* helps
   the youth know one another better.

Rituals and Other Faith Practices

Rituals, even simple ones, form persons (body and all) into common patterns of communal identity with the community of faith.

- Regularly sing "Happy Birthday," join hands for closing prayer, or sing a benediction together.
- Invite youth to lead a regular (if brief) period of worship each week.
- Offer simple food. Lovingly prepared, healthful food—even snacks—draws persons together.
- Practice the faith together. After a series on hunger, challenge the class to serve dinner and lead worship at a local shelter.

Curriculum:
A Point of Departure

Curriculum is a plan
or framework
for how learning
should proceed.

Having a curriculum is better than not having one, but the perfect curriculum has not yet been invented. Any curriculum should, therefore, be flexible and adaptive.

Most denominations print their own curriculum resources, including material for youth. Some denominations have resource persons to train local congregations in the use of these resources. Check with pastors or denominational leaders to inquire about these services.

Printed curriculum, especially the kind published by denominations, has over time become the favorite whipping post for every problem in the Sunday school. It is variously judged

- **too deep, too shallow,**
- **too biblical, too topical;**
- **too conventional,
  too innovative;**
- **overly sensitive to diversity,
  insensitive to diversity;**
- **and, well, you get the idea.**

Criticism of curriculum resources may be justified. But we may also be asking the wrong questions about resources. Do we see resources as an end, instead of a means? Do we ask too much of resources, because we are more concerned about doing the teaching than about being a teacher?

An interesting point: Experienced and effective Sunday school teachers are both more positive in their assessment of resources and less dependent on them. They use resources as a point of departure but breathe into the printed pages a wealth of lived Christian experience. It's funny how Christ carriers make a decent curriculum resource extraordinary!

Denominational vs. Independent Curriculum

In general, you can expect denominational curriculum to be theologically safe and educationally sound, though not always the flashiest car on the lot. Denominational publishers are saddled with many, sometimes competing, responsibilities and limited resources. Denominational curriculum strives for substance but is occasionally forced to fudge a little on novelty and form.

Independent curriculum requires some checking on the theological perspective. Independent publishers may spend more on color, art, and glossy paper. These resources often tout being easy to teach or needing no preparation. Please note that **all resources require preparation**—just gathering all of the materials called for by some no-preparation resources would take 30–45 minutes!

PREPARE!

Curriculum and Learning Activities

Some teachers ask: "Why do I need curriculum? It never gets to the point. Let me just teach my subject without the frills."

Most often this kind of teaching means lecturing. Lecturing is fine for students who learn best by hearing. But not all do.

Some learn best by discussing,
others by acting out or simulating an experience,
others by reading,
others by using their gifts for the arts.

Some are solitary learners,
some learn better through group interaction,
some learn best when they are moved emotionally.

For any given subgroup of a class, specific activities embody the point. Skip the artsy frill, and somebody might not connect with your theme. Good curriculum always holds the variety of teaching and learning styles in mind and counters teachers' tendencies to rely on their own particular style at the expense of all others.

The Unspoken Curriculum

- Is the meeting space bright and cheery or dark and dank? Is it located this side of Jerusalem?
- Are students made to feel welcome when they arrive or ignored?
- Whose voices are heard most often, males or females?
- Are Bibles available to all or only to the teacher?
- If attendance is down, does the teacher focus on the absentees or those present?
- Are student questions encouraged or dismissed as interruptions?
- How old are the posters on the wall?
- How much of the things mentioned above can you change today?

Each of these classroom dynamics (and there are many more) teaches a great deal, especially about realities of power in the lives of youth.

Sometimes this unspoken curriculum actually subverts a church's stated commitment to youth as full partners in ministry.

The Culture Has a Curriculum Too

Consumption and competition are culture's principal lessons. Youth have mastered this curriculum. They are expert at reading the trappings of status: clothing, school affiliation, cars, college acceptance.

Exposing this cultural curriculum as a lie is crucial if Christian faith is to be lived with integrity.

20 Terrific Teaching Tips

Pedagogy for the Practical and Pragmatic

Teaching is first and foremost an expression of the teacher's character and not technique. However, teachers of character are always looking for ways to improve their skills. **These are CPR things you can do right away to improve the quality of your class.**

The suggestions that follow take seriously that people like to learn in different ways. It also takes seriously the reality that Sunday school is not just facts, but skills for making meaning at the intersection of faith and life.

1 CREATE BANNERS

Hang shelf paper, butcher paper or computer paper on a wall and encourage youth to draw a scene, story, verse or theme. A wise teacher of middle schoolers suggests covering tables with paper and encouraging students to doodle something related to the theme or topic during class.

2 PLAY SIMULATION GAMES

Set up a situation, assign roles, and ask groups to negotiate a solution. For example, in a simulation on world food distribution, serve 10 percent of the class a full breakfast, 70 percent rice cakes, and the remaining 20 percent nothing at all. Wait two minutes for righteous indignation to foment (or ferment), then ask the groups how they are going to solve the problem.

3 BRAINSTORM

Generate lists: means of grace, modes of biblical transportation, heroes and villains from church history, talking animals of the Old Testament, whatever!

Brainstorming is lively fun, with the advantage that everyone's idea get written on newsprint or chalkboard. Then do some critical thinking about the lists. Some things won't work; some are easier to do; some need to be listed by priority.

4 HERO, VICTIM, FOOL

Present a list of names of persons that youth will know. Ask youth to identify each person as a hero, a victim, or a fool and to explain why. Vote on each person's status, and discuss reactions. Talk about the utility and pitfalls of stereotyping. Naturally, you do not name anyone who might be hurt by this process.

5 DECIDE IF IT'S OK OR NOT OK

Describe brief vignettes that include moral tension. Ask students to vote their feelings on the moral issues brought up in the vignette, then discuss them. Example: A married man with a family is convicted the second time for drunk driving. His conviction is overturned, and he gets to keep his license because he needs the car for work.

6 FIND THINGS IN COMMON

Divide the youth into small groups and provide pencils and paper. Allow five minutes to for them to generate lists of common likes or dislikes in specific categories (food, school subjects, TV shows). An item may be added to the list only when all members of the group agree that they either like or dislike the item.

7 USE VARIATIONS OF THE OPINION POLL

Walk the Line—Hang signs with the words *Agree* and *Disagree* on opposite walls of the room. Point out the invisible yet real continuum in the open space between the signs. Make up statements about which youth might have opinions or might quickly form opinions, such as "The Bible is 100 percent factual." Then ask the youth to place their bodies somewhere on the continuum. Ask persons at different points on the continuum to explain their positions. (This activity works well with active middle schoolers—and with blasé senior highs.)

Take a Stand—A more laid-back version of Walk the Line. Zero fingers (2 balled fists) represents strong disagreement, ten fingers represents strong agreement. Five fingers is in the middle. Have youth consider for a moment a statement such as "All talking animals in the Old Testament are well informed." Then have the youth flash a finger count when the leader says, "Take a stand!" Have advocates of different stances defend their positions. (This activity works well with senior highs concerned with keeping physical activity to an absolute minimum.)

8 DISCUSS THE BIG ISSUES

In many cases, youth care, but think that they can't help. Use this activity to present the big issues like hunger or peace and to develop realistic and rational strategies where none seem possible. Brainstorm a list of barriers and reachable steps; then analyze them. Look for smaller or more local goals that would support the larger one. Then develop an action plan to accomplish the goals.

9 PLAN WITH THE CLASS

Youth are likely to have a higher investment in the class if they have a part in the planning. This requires extra work on the part of the leader, but the results are well worth the investment.

10 EMPLOY TECHNOLOGY

Youth do not suffer from the techno-phobia, otherwise known as Flashing 12:00 Syndrome, that adults sometimes do. Put tape recorders, video recorders, and computers in their hands and tell them to create. The possibilities are endless. This requires careful planning and preparation, but the payoff is humongous!

11 ACT IT OUT

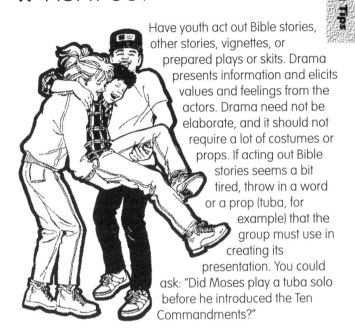

Have youth act out Bible stories, other stories, vignettes, or prepared plays or skits. Drama presents information and elicits values and feelings from the actors. Drama need not be elaborate, and it should not require a lot of costumes or props. If acting out Bible stories seems a bit tired, throw in a word or a prop (tuba, for example) that the group must use in creating its presentation. You could ask: "Did Moses play a tuba solo before he introduced the Ten Commandments?"

12 POSE

Ask youth to strike a pose or place another youth in a pose that best demonstrates the feeling or behavior of a character in a particular situation or story.

13 CHECK THE TEMPERATURE

Use this activity to test how things are going. Ask: "Are we hot or cold? Which should we be? How can we get there?" Use this test for appreciation, new information, hopes and wishes, concerns, or puzzlements. Categories will help youth discover what they are thinking and what others are thinking without getting bogged down in concerns and complaints.

14 COMPARE TEXTS OF THE BIBLE

Using different versions of the Bible, compare how the same passages are alike or different. Ask the following questions:

Does the wording change the implied or stated message?

Does a change in punctuation emphasize one idea over another?

Do the words used carry different connotations from one version to another?

What does this exercise teach about biblical interpretation?

15 ENCOURAGE YOUTH LEADERSHIP

Youth may take on part or all of the responsibility for teaching any given session. Depending on the teaching task, this will require appropriate preplanning with adult leaders. Student teachers should be given the opportunity to debrief their experiences. After the session, ask questions such as "How did it feel to be on the other side of the podium?"

16 USE READERS THEATRE

Youth will read a play, Bible story, or narrative in character, using their voices dramatically and with minimal gestures. Skip the "he saids" and "she addeds." Include a narrator to read the descriptions of action. This is an excellent way to hold attention through long passages of Scripture.

17 TELL STORIES

Human beings are created to hear and tell stories. Use stories from the Bible, the tradition of the church, your own local church's tradition, and contemporary life.

18 KEEP RITUALS AND SACRAMENTS

Rituals are repeated patterns of behavior that carry a people's memories, stories, and beliefs through embodied, symbolic action. For Protestants, until recently, the adjective most often associated with ritual was *empty*. We all know that works, including ritual works, can't save; but we have begun to realize how effective (and important) rituals—including the sacraments—are for bearing the deepest truths of our identity. Ask youth to reflect on the rituals in their homes—birthdays, Christmas, Easter, Thanksgiving, the first day of school. How do families spend these holidays? What purpose do holiday rituals serve? Would Thanksgiving be Thanksgiving without the meal? Why or why not?

Create and use a ritual as a class.

19 AROUSE CURIOSITY

Rearrange the chairs in the room. Use the walls to post clues to the Scripture verse or Bible character for the day. Put the materials for a learning activity in the center of a table. Do something different—the more unusual, the better. When youth enter the room, they'll want to know what's going to happen. Curiosity may kill cats, but it helps youth learn.

20 LECTURE

OK, there is a place for the occasional lecture. Since youth can't reflect on what they don't know, a lecture is an efficient way to convey new information. A good lecture is systematic, well illustrated, and brief. It is not an hour-long ramble through the teacher's stream of consciousness, nor is it a failed discussion. Let us avoid at all costs the example of Ferris Buehler's hopelessly pathetic history teacher, who droned for an hour, stopping only to ask, then answering his own pointless questions: "Class? Anyone?" Class lecture should complement a variety of learning methods in a teaching plan.

10 Things Wise Sunday School Teachers Know

1 TO CARE IS TO PREPARE

Last-minute, cut-short preparation says, "I don t care enough about my students to prepare a lesson. Nor do I care enough about the faith to want to present it in an appealing way."

2 PHYSICAL MATURITY IS ONLY THE TIP OF THE ICEBERG

The visible physical changes of puberty usually precede and sometimes mask the emergence of equally dramatic, but less visible, capacities for cognitive understanding, emotional engagement, and social interaction.

3 MIDDLE SCHOOLERS NEED TO MOVE TO LEARN

Asking youth to sit still for an hour is like asking flies not to buzz.

4 GIRLS NEED ATTENTION

Research continues to find that adolescent girls come to view their own gifts and attributes of character less highly than do males. Teachers must take special care to honor the contributions and giftedness of female students.

5 SKILL DEVELOPMENT IS NOT AUTOMATIC

The emerging capacities for cognition, emotion, and social interaction make possible abstractions of logic, understanding another's point of view, valuing the approval of peers, having mind and heart tickled by metaphor, experiencing the power of religious symbols, and weaving the biblical story into the story of one's life. Taken together, these represent a qualitatively different way of constructing the world and the self from, say, the imperialistic self-centeredness of childhood. But these skills are not passed out with driver's licenses at the DMV. Capacities become skills only in an environment that seeks to nurture them.

6 THE FAITHFUL MUST BE TAUGHT TO WORSHIP

The power of God to meet and form a people through worship depends on the people's capacity to respond. Our capacity to worship may be innate, but it must also be nurtured. Teaching about worship, using worship tools such as hymnals and worship books, and worshiping together in the classroom are important. Resist the temptation to skip learning activities about worship as unrelated to Sunday school. And ask a youth to help you carry all those hymnals to and from the sanctuary.

7 TEACHERS TEACH PERSONS NOT CONTENT

We teach the faith for the transformation of lives.

8 REAL LIFE IS RARELY SO ORDERLY AS THE MIND OF PIAGET

Developmental categories—childhood, early adolescence, late adolescence—and their lists of criteria are descriptive for youth in general but almost never of a particular teenager.

9 BENEFITS DON'T ALWAYS HAPPEN OVERNIGHT

Sometimes a former student, who seemed indifferent to all of your effort, will surprise and delight you years later with the fruit of a seed that he or she claims that you planted.

10 PRAY, AND TRUST THE SPIRIT

This needs no explanation.

Remembering, Not Forgetting: How Stories Form God's People

This workshop is designed for youth Sunday school teachers and administrators but could be adapted to include youth as well. The purposes are to

- reaffirm the importance of teachers in the church's ministry with youth;
- link the teaching task to storytelling and faith formation;
- discover practical helps for teaching.

The workshop also models effective teaching methods. The workshop facilitator(s) may wish to pause on occasion to reflect on these methods. Questions such as "What did we just do here? How does the technique support the learning? Why this exercise now?" should help generate discussion.

WELCOME (5 minutes)

This might include a greeting, brief expressions of gratitude and affirmation for ministry with youth, an appropriate hymn or song, and prayer.

SHARING MY STORY (20 minutes)

Ahead of time, write the following statements on newsprint or chalkboard:

The Short Story of My Life

When I was a child, I _____.

During adolescence, I _____ and I also _____ a lot, too.

The best part of my teen years was _____ _____.

The worst part was _____.

I knew that I was really an adult when ____ _____.

Throughout my life, God has _____ _____.

The facilitator may wish to tell her or his own story first to model for the group. An upbeat tone, but not to the exclusion of honest disclosure, is best. If your group is large, divide the group into smaller groups of four. The person whose birthday is closest to today should begin.

When the groups are finished talking, ask:
- What made your adolescence different from your childhood? your adulthood?
- How has God's loving claim on and guidance in your life become clearer to you as you have grown in age and experience?
- In what sense has God's Story (whatever you understand that phrase to mean) shaped the writing of your own life story?

FORGETTING AND REMEMBERING: A BIBLICAL PERSPECTIVE ON THE IMPORTANCE OF STORIES

(30 minutes)

Read 2 Kings 22–23:3 as a Readers Theatre (see page 55 for directions).

Assign the following parts to persons who enjoy reading publicly: Narrator, King Josiah, Shaphan, Hilkiah, Huldah.

After the reading make sure that everyone understands the narrative. Explain to the group that scholars believe that the scroll found in the Temple was the earliest version of the Book of Deuteronomy. They believe this to be the case based on the reforms Josiah enacts in Chapter 23. It was likely found in an old money chest or perhaps inside a newly exposed wall frame. Point out the extraordinary literary quality of this narrative with, for example, the almost comedic imagery of burly-armed, tool-belted construction workers clunking around the Temple, creating plaster-dust clouds and piles of rubble everywhere juxtaposed to the dramatic understatement of Shaphan's words to the king: "Hilkiah the priest has given me a book."

Then assign the following passages to group members: Deuteronomy 23:4, 5, 6, 7, 10, 11, 21-23, 24.

Ask them to read their passage and be prepared to relate to the others (1) what practices had been ongoing in and around Judah up to the time of the recovery of this Book of Deuteronomy and (2) what specific reforms Judah enacted based on the book. List these findings in two columns on a chalkboard or newsprint.

After the results are posted, ask:

- According to the writers of 2 Kings, what had God's People lost as a result of losing this scroll? (knowledge of specific laws and worshiping practices, but more fundamentally, their memories of God's history of covenant care for them.)

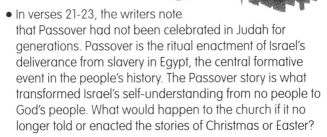

- How are a community's memories tied to its sense of identity?

- In verses 21-23, the writers note that Passover had not been celebrated in Judah for generations. Passover is the ritual enactment of Israel's deliverance from slavery in Egypt, the central formative event in the people's history. The Passover story is what transformed Israel's self-understanding from no people to God's people. What would happen to the church if it no longer told or enacted the stories of Christmas or Easter?

- What implications does this story have for the church's ministry with youth? for Sunday school?

HELPING YOUTH ENCOUNTER THE STORIES

(30 minutes)

Ahead of time, write the following on newsprint or on a chalkboard:

Ingredients for Sunday School

- Bible study
- discussion of important topics of interest or concern
- learning the traditions of denomination and church
- safe forum for questions
- teaching skills
- teacher as role model
- curriculum
- understanding adolescent needs and gifts
- worshiping and learning about worship
- meeting space and time
- relationships

Say: Youth are becoming developmentally capable of understanding and telling their lives as a story. The church believes that the most significant gift and resource it can provide for youth in this telling is a relationship with Jesus Christ. Sunday school can be a crucial forum for youth to build and strengthen that relationship—that is, for the story of God to become central to youth's own stories. Look at the list of possible ingredients that go into a youth Sunday school class.

Ask: "Are there other ingredients you would add?"

Ask participants individually to rank these ingredients in order of importance. Then discuss the differences in rankings and priorities.

Then ask participants to rank the ingredients in terms of perceived effectiveness. What ingredients in their classes are most effective? least effective? Why?

If, in the discussion of this last set of questions, a theme emerges, direct participants to the appropriate sections in this guide as a means for further exploration and discussion. For example, common concerns about curriculum can be explored by turning to the section on curriculum on pages 41–46. If a variety of themes emerges, participants may gather in small groups to discuss their particular interests. Use the questions and comments in the relevant sections of this book as guides for discussions.

If the group decides that they need to do some serious research, refer to Sunday School Check-Up on pages 17–23. Suggest that this gathering might be the first step toward evaluation, reform, and renewal of the church's educational ministry with youth.

CLOSING (5 Minutes)

- Read together your congregation's promise to the newly baptized from your church's baptismal ritual.
- Thank teachers for their faithfulness to their baptismal covenant.
- Pray for youth to become living stories of God's love.

THE BIG PICTURE

Working with youth is a little like putting together a jigsaw puzzle: It helps to have a picture of what it's supposed to look like! (See page 73.)

In effective youth ministry **vision** is central.

Seven major elements contribute to realizing that vision. The more of them that are developed and in place, the better.

Youth ministry planners in individual churches can develop each of those areas **their own way**, according to their congregation's particular resources, gifts, and priorities and the needs of their youth.

How does this SkillAbility fit in this big picture? Here are just a few of the ways. By using ideas in this book, not only do you build up the value and attractiveness of your youth Sunday school, you also

- create an **ETHOS** that says Sunday school is an exciting, caring, and important part of life

- create **STRUCTURE** that will help build Sunday school long term as a tool for forming faith, fostering identity, and making meaning

- enrich youth **EXPERIENCES** and comfort zone in learning the Word and living the faith.

YOUTH MINISTRY: A COMPREHENSIVE APPROACH

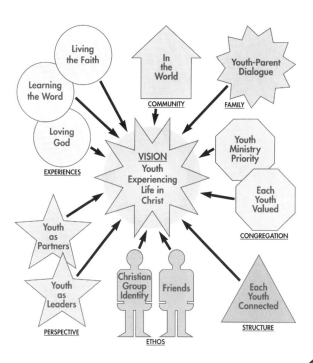

FAMILY

Research is clear that **parent-youth dialogue** about matters of faith is crucial for youth to develop mature faith. Youth themselves express desire to be listened to, to have boundaries, and to have parental involvement in their lives. Parents need skills for relating to their changing teens as well as assurance that their values and voice do matter to their youth. How do we in the church facilitate parent-youth dialogue?

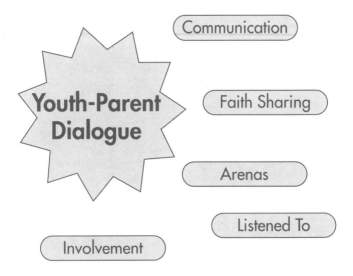

Youth-Parent Dialogue

Communication

Faith Sharing

Arenas

Listened To

Involvement

CONGREGATION

Youth ministry is the ministry of the whole congregation, beginning with making **youth ministry a priority**: prayer for the ministry, people (not just one person), time, effort, training, resources, and funding. The goal for the congregation is **each youth valued**. Interaction with adults, including mentors, positive language about youth, prayer partners for each one, simply being paid attention to—these are active roles for the congregation.

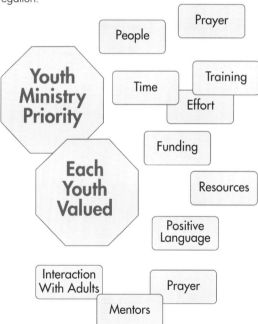

STRUCTURE

Whatever shape the ministry takes, the goal is to have **each youth connected**. Sunday school and youth group are only a beginning. What are the needs of the youth? What groups (even of only 2 or 3 youth) and what times would help connect young people to the faith community? How easy is it for new youth to enter? How well do we stay in touch with the changing needs of our youth? Do we have structures in place that facilitate communication? outreach? "How" can vary; it's the "why" that's crucial.

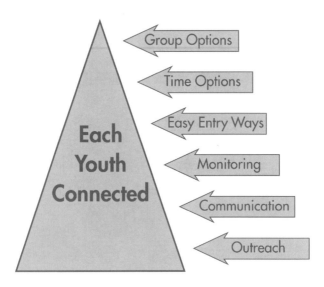

Group Options

Time Options

Easy Entry Ways

Monitoring

Communication

Outreach

Each Youth Connected

ETHOS

We are relational beings; we all need **friends**. The support, caring, and accountability friends provide help youth experience the love of God. As those friendships are nurtured within **Christian group identity**, young people claim for themselves a personal identity of being Christian. What language, rituals, traditions, and bonding experiences mark each grouping within the youth ministry as distinctively Christian?

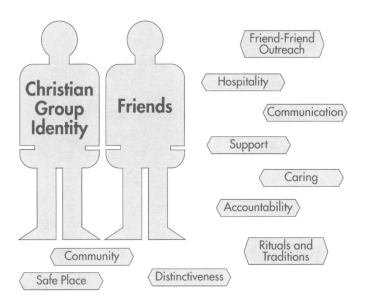

Christian Group Identity

Friends

Friend-Friend Outreach

Hospitality

Communication

Support

Caring

Accountability

Rituals and Traditions

Community

Safe Place

Distinctiveness

PERSPECTIVE

Youth are keenly aware of being seen as problems, being treated as objects to be fixed, or as recipients too inexperienced to have anything to offer. What would happen if we operated from the perspective of seeing **youth as leaders, youth as partners**? We would listen to them more, be intentional about identifying their gifts, take seriously their input, encourage their decision making, and train them for leadership roles.

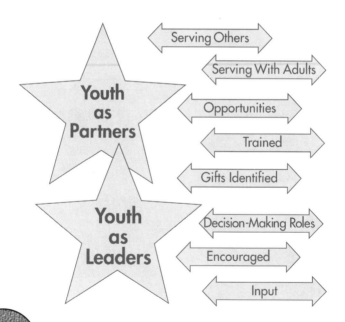

EXPERIENCES

Worship, devotions, prayer, and participation in the community of faith build for youth the experience of **loving God**. Study and reflection upon the Bible and the faith are crucial for **learning the Word**. Being among people who are Christian role models and grappling with difficult moral, ethical, justice, and stewardship issues help young people with **living the faith**. Curriculum resources specifically provide material to facilitate these three kinds of experiences.

COMMUNITY

As Christians, youth are challenged to be **in the world** as servants, as witnesses, as leaven—making a difference with their lives, giving others a glimpse of the Kingdom. What opportunities, what training, what support do we give youth to equip them for ministry beyond the walls of the church building?

In the World

Serving

Witnessing

Leaven/Salt/Light